DOODLE AND DECIDE
COLORING MEDITATION TO AWAKEN INTUITION

a companion to
DECISION DEXTERITY

Original artwork by Lynn Marie of Rosewater Tattoo.
Images are designed to correspond with Decision Dexterity methodology.

Channeled meditations via Octavia Brooks, Intuitive Relationship Expert for Entrepreneurs.

Decision Journey exercises are by Terrie Novak as a companion to Decision Dexterity publications and online course.

Copyright © 2021 by Terrie Novak
All rights reserved
ISBN: 978-1-7331588-1-7
Published by Concept Bridges, LLC
Tigard, Oregon 97224

No part of this publication may be reproduced, stored in a retrieval system, or transmitted in any form or by any means electronic, mechanical, photocopying, recording, scanning or otherwise, except as permitted under section 107 or 108 of the 1976 United States Copyright Act without the prior written permission of the publisher via the author.

www.terrienovak.com

COLORING MEDITATION

Woman with Universe

I am seeing from my new eyes. I am seeing with my Star Eyes.

Green Man

The blooming of my soul is the blossoming of my heart.

Order in Chaos

I avail myself to all the choices.

Growth in Decay

I trust myself with my emotions.

Guided Pattern

I have a new framework called expansion.

Bright and Bold

I put a loving voice into the world.

Woman with Universe

I am seeing from my new eyes. I am seeing with my Star Eyes.

Green Man

The blooming of my soul is the blossoming of my heart.

Order in Chaos

I avail myself to all the choices.

Growth in Decay

I trust myself with my emotions.

Guided Pattern

I have a new framework called expansion.

Bright and Bold

I put a loving voice into the world.

DECISION JOURNEY NOTEBOOK

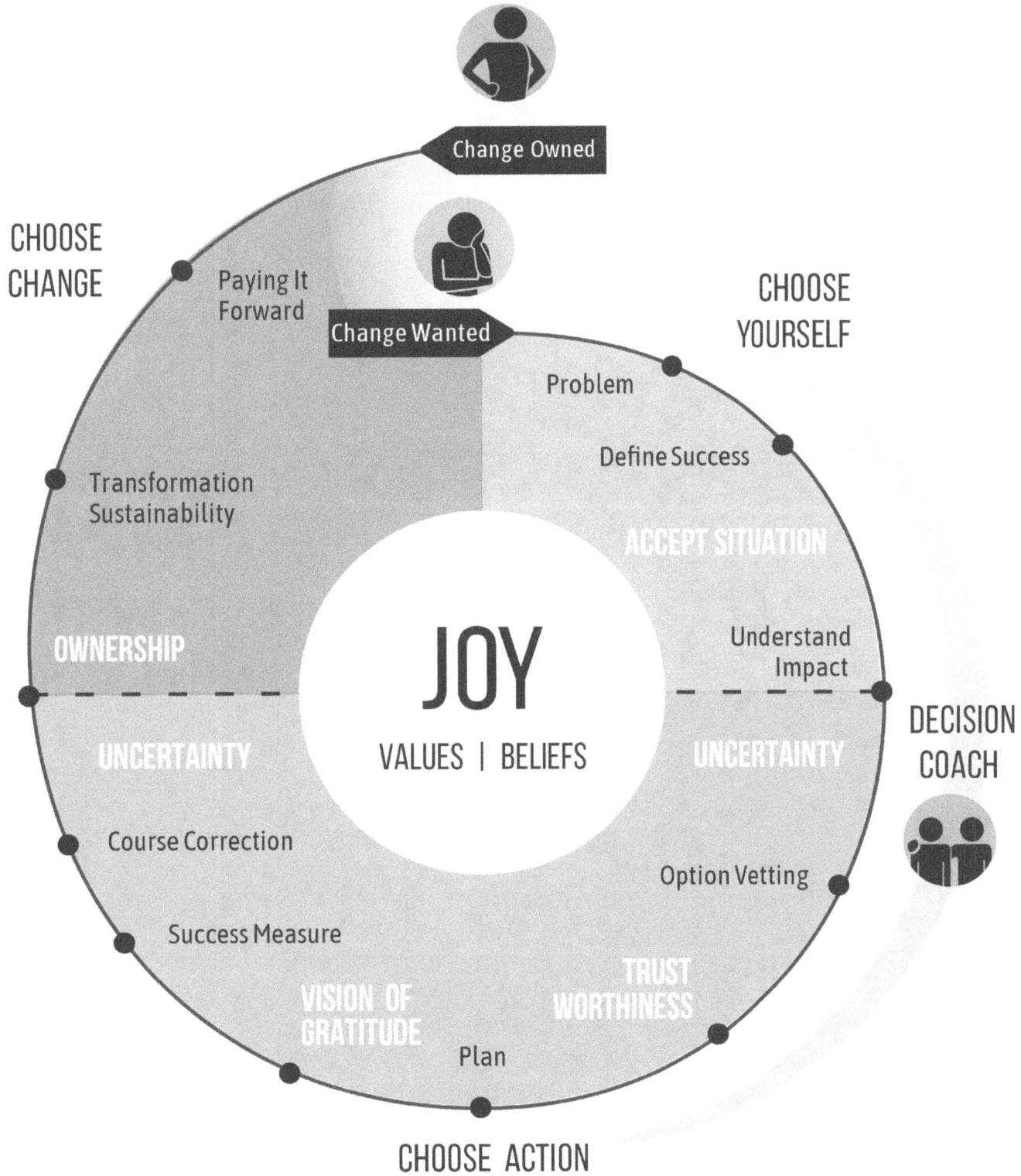

 # QUIZ – What's your Decision Dexterity?

Rate your decision-making now. Reevaluate after 7 days of practicing the following decision-making methods. Did your Decision Dexterity grow?

1= Never thought about it, don't do it   5= I always do this

	1	2	3	4	5
CHOOSE SELF					
I understand the problem that drove me to this decision point.					
I know and accept my current situation, including any constraints involved.					
I know and accept my preferences in what I want, believe, and value in this topic.					
I know what makes me feel alive and joyful about this topic.					
I know what I a fear about this topic.					
I validated my assumptions about this topic.					
I know what the successful result looks like and know how to measure my progress.					

	1	2	3	4	5
CHOOSE ACTION					
I search for information that extends beyond my social group and current perspective.					
I identified many relevant options, from sources that are trustworthy.					
I evaluated options against my preferences and success measures, so I know the valid options will solve the problem.					
I understand the impact of the options I selected, both to myself and others.					
I track my reasoning for rejecting options.					
I share my thinking with an objective person I trust, they give me immediate feedback.					
I made a simple plan of action.					
I imagined what it might look like if there was a bad outcome and altered my action plan to include activities to detect and prevent that from happening.					

	1	2	3	4	5
CHOOSE CHANGE					
I follow a decision process, so I keep moving forward during uncertainty.					
I follow my action plan and periodically measure progress, so I can course correct as needed.					
I envision what it would be like to live with the results and include any activities needed for me to be ready for achieving and sustaining the results.					
I know what makes me feel alive and joyful about this topic.					
I am confident and have the energy to move forward with activities that bring this change.					

	1	2	3	4	5
INTUITIVE THINKING					
I use both critical thinking and intuitive thinking throughout the series of decisions.					
I intentionally quiet my body and mind to call in intuition before making a big decision.					
I have a favorite place or activity I use daily for calming my mind.					
I track when I use intuition in my decisions and note the outcome of those decisions.					
I acknowledge decisions I am grateful for every day.					
I recognize when my intuition is signaling me.					
I trust my inner voice and act on it.					

PROBLEM DEFINITION – Play 20 questions.

Bring to mind that tough decision and write down your honest answers.

1	Was there an event that triggered this need?	
2	Is this problem a surprise? What is surprising or familiar about it?	
3	What are you most concerned about?	
4	Can you observe or measure the concerns? How is that compared to what it should be.	
5	How often or persistent it the problem?	
6	How long has this been known to be happening?	
7	How do you see yourself now with this happening? How do you think others see you?	
8	Who else is involved and what are their concerns? How are they impacted?	
9	Who's concerns matter if you chose to address this problem?	
10	What emotions does this problem bring up in you or those around you?	

 PROBLEM DEFINITION – Play 20 questions.

11	Why do you think these concerns exist? And then ask why about that answer a few more times.	
12	How are you taking care of this situation now?	
13	Is there something you know about what's happening that you typically don't tell others? What is that? Why is that?	
14	Is this problem preventing you from doing something else you've always wanted to do?	
15	Is there a time when you need this resolved by?	
16	Is there anything else constraining what you can do for this problem (money, people, regulations, your beliefs, someone else's beliefs?)	
17	What would happen if nothing was done about it?	
18	Can this problem go away on their own?	
19	Why has nothing been done before now?	
20	Are there any obvious or known solutions?	

# SUCCESS CRITERIA – What does it look like to be wildly successful?

Do this discovery exercise *immediately* after the problem definition.
Pro tip: quantify so you can measure your progress.

1	What will you have/not have? Is there something you want so deeply you just *know* it's going to happen?	
2	How will you know when you have it?	
3	Is there something you just know, so deeply, that you are sure it's going to happen?	
4	Is there something you just know absolutely must *not* happen?	
5	When do you think you'll have the result?	
6	How will you see yourself?	
7	How will others see you?	
8	How will you feel?	
9	Who will you be thanking?	
10	What will it look like once the results are part of your new life as usual? Create a brief story of 'a day in your life'.	

 # PREFERENCES – Do you understand the impact of your decision?

What do you need to get from where you are now, to where you want to be?

		Bridge the gap from current to desired.	*My values and beliefs.*
1		What are my values and beliefs on this topic?	My credo.
2		Do I need help getting from where I am now to where I want to be?	My capabilities and resources
3		Are there known solutions I can use to get my desired results? Who owns or knows how to build the solution?	Known solution providers
4		Is there a time when I must arrive? What pace am I willing to move?	Pace and timing
5		What do I need to be safe while in transition?	Personal safety
6		How do I want to let people know I am making this change?	Announcements
7		What do I need to bring with me? What do I need to leave behind?	Practices and possessions
8		Who around me now will be affected when I attain the results?	Current relationships
9		Do you have everything I need to successfully live with the results?	Readiness
10		What are my expectations of the people and conditions once I arrive?	Future relationships

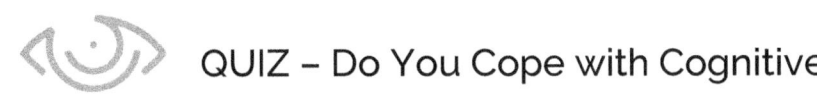

QUIZ – Do You Cope with Cognitive Bias?

Rate how you cope with your own cognitive bias.

1= Never thought about it, don't do it   5= I always do this

	1	2	3	4	5
SELF-KNOWLEDGE BASELINE					
I understand the problem that drove me to this decision point.					
I know what I a fear about this topic.					
I know my values and believes on this topic and what makes me feel alive and joyful about it.					
I know what the successful result looks like and know how to measure my progress.					
I know and accept my current situation, including any constraints involved.					
I considered what I would have my best friend do if this was their decision.					

	1	2	3	4	5
THINKING AND FEELING					
I avoid acting based on *reaction* and allow myself to Think-Feel-Choose- and then Act.					
I call on intuition before deciding and have established a place I go where I call on my intuition.					
I encourage divergent thinking (one way is to take a walk while thinking).					
I have a curious attitude (this improves creative problem-solving, tolerance, openness, inquisitiveness).					
I manage my brain's response to uncertainty by following a decision process (Choose You, Choose Action, Choose Change).					
I ask a decision coach to be my advocate and provide real-time bias feedback.					

	1	2	3	4	5
BENCHMARKING					
I practice decision and intuition benchmarking by keeping a journal of my decisions.					
I track my reasoning for rejecting options.					
I imagined what it might look like if there was a bad outcome (pre-mortem) and altered my action plan to include activities to detect and prevent that from happening.					
I performed a 12 question decision quality review to check for bias in the action plan.					

OPTION VETTING WORKSHEET

Do your research findings align with your beliefs?

	Option Title	Addresses Problem?	Delivers success criteria?	Aligns with preferences?	Do you choose to go forward with this option?
✏️	Describe option	Yes or No	Yes or No	Yes or No	Describe why
1					
2					
3					
4					
5					

 PLAN OF ACTION

Are you ready to navigate uncertainty?

1	**START** When will you start acting on your decision?	
2	**ACTION** What are the significant tasks, events, or milestones?	
3	**JOY CENTERED** What activities will you include that bring you joy and keep you moving forward?	
4	**GRATITUDE** What thank-you moments will you have to honor those helping you make this change? Practice gratitude every day by visualizing that feeling you will have when the results are part of your life.	
5	**MEASURE PROGRESS** How will you measure your progress towards success? How will this support any needed course corrections?	
6	**COMMUNICATION** Who will you tell about this change? How will you tell them?	
7	**RESULTS** How will you know when you are done? When you've realized all of your success criteria, how will you feel?	

DECISION QUALITY REVIEW – Noble prize-winning advice

Use this quality review to check your plan of action for cognitive bias. Update your plan as needed.

1	Ask the decision maker.	Is anyone involved to date motivated by self-interest?
2		Are the people making recommendations minimizing risks or exaggerating benefits?
3		If there were contradictory recommendations, were the conflicts explored sufficiently?
4	Ask those recommending solution options.	Were recommendations based on past success stories? If yes, the comparisons might not be valid to the current situation.
5		Have viable alternatives been offered and evaluated? Imagine you had to make this decision *again* in a year. Is there more information you would want? If yes, see if you can get it now.
6		If numbers were involved, do you know where they came from and which were facts versus which were estimates? What were the estimates based on?
7		Was the person providing the recommendation branded as 'excellent'? Does what made them great apply to your situation?
8		Was the person providing the recommendation already heavily invested in their approach? If the previous history didn't exist, would this still be the recommendation?
9	Evaluate the proposed action plan.	Does it sound overly optimistic? Does it sound like they are on a 'winning streak'? Is the plan overly cautious?
10		Has the plan been compared at all to similar historic plans?
11		Has there been consideration for the effect or impact the change will have after it's realized? Are any negative reactions anticipated?
12		Was a pre-mortem carried out? Did it prompt any changes to the recommended plan?

Resource: Kahneman, Lovallo, Sibony, June 2011 Harvard Business Review https://hbr.org/2011/06/the-big-idea-before-you-make-that-big-decision

Decision Dexterity Copyright ©2021 by Terrie Novak
Published by Concept Bridges, LLC

DECISION COACHING – What to expect

When a friend asks for help with a tough decision, they are counting on you to balance their brain's response to uncertainty.

A decision coach:

1	Does *not* make the decision for you.
2	Helps you define and communicate success criteria & preferences.
3	Acts as an objective sounding board to help you recognize when cognitive bias is affecting your decision.
4	Encourages you to trust your intuition and advises when to use it.
5	Keeps you focused on what's important by creating a plan of action and encouraging you to reference it.
6	Helps you understand what's involved in owning the outcome.
7	May perform agreed upon tasks for you, as you adjust to the transition.

 INTUITION BENCHMARK CARDS – Prove your decisions are trustworthy

I'm so happy I decided to...

✏ _____
my decision

✏ _____
aligned with this belief

✏ _____
my critical thinking in this decision

✏ _____
my inner voice in this decision

Outcome _____

I'm so happy I decided to...

✏ _____
my decision

✏ _____
aligns with this belief

✏ _____
my critical thinking in this decision

✏ _____
my inner voice in this decision

Outcome _____

I'm so happy I decided to...

✏ _____
my decision

✏ _____
aligned with this belief

✏ _____
my critical thinking in this decision

✏ _____
my inner voice in this decision

Outcome _____

I'm so happy I decided to...

✏ _____
my decision

✏ _____
aligns with this belief

✏ _____
my critical thinking in this decision

✏ _____
my inner voice in this decision

Outcome _____

 INTUITION BENCHMARK CARDS – Prove your decisions are trustworthy

---

I'm so happy I decided to...

✎ _____
my decision

✎ _____
aligned with this belief

✎ _____
my critical thinking in this decision

✎ _____
my inner voice in this decision

Outcome _____

I'm so happy I decided to...

✎ _____
my decision

✎ _____
aligns with this belief

✎ _____
my critical thinking in this decision

✎ _____
my inner voice in this decision

Outcome _____

I'm so happy I decided to...

✎ _____
my decision

✎ _____
aligned with this belief

✎ _____
my critical thinking in this decision

✎ _____
my inner voice in this decision

Outcome _____

I'm so happy I decided to...

✎ _____
my decision

✎ _____
aligns with this belief

✎ _____
my critical thinking in this decision

✎ _____
my inner voice in this decision

Outcome _____

 ONLINE COURSE – Choose lessons that answer your burning questions

Mark and prioritize lessons that answer most commonly asked questions and address your learning goals.
Enroll @terrienovak.com

	Top priority	Sounds interesting	Maybe later
Introduction: How will this course transform me?			
How do I progress through lessons and get the most out of this course?			
How can I get 1:1 decision coaching?			
Lesson 1: System of decision making			
What is a process?			
What is the system of decision-making?			
When is it important for me to make decisions for myself?			
Is it ok for me to decide based on a gut feeling?			
What is the system of decision-making?			
How does intuition work in decision-making?			
What do I do when I have to choose between what's right and what's easy?			
Lesson 2: Decision making traps			
Is feeling fear of decisions normal?			
Can the way I think lead to bad decisions?			
Is social media working against me when I make decisions?			
How can I avoid decision making traps?			
How do I evaluate digital information?			
Lesson 3: Bias busting toolkit			
What tools can I keep in my back pocket when facing tough decisions?			
Is it even possible to know what I don't know?			
What should I expect from someone I am counting on the help me make decisions?			
How can I help my customer make timely decisions?			
Lesson 4: CHOOSE YOU define self-knowledge baseline			
How can I tell if I am making a good decision?			
Are decisions actions?			
Is it important I understand the problem, even if I don't feel like I have one?			
How do I know what success looks like?			
What can I proactively do to make decisions feel easier?			
How can knowing my credo help me make decisions faster?			
How do I know if I can do this?			
Can I tell if I am making a bad decision?			

 # ONLINE COURSE – Choose lessons that answer your burning questions

Mark and prioritize lessons that answer most commonly asked questions and address your learning goals.
Enroll @terrienovak.com

	Top priority	Sounds interesting	Maybe later
Lesson 5: Cultivate intuition and trust			
How can I make decisions faster using intuition?			
Does decision making become easier with practice?			
How can I be ready for intuition?			
What does intuition feel like?			
Can I learn to trust my intuition?			
Why does indecision have to be so agonizing?			
What can I do to resolve my love/hate relationship with journaling?			
Can I trust information I read online?			
How can I avoid analysis paralysis?			
Lesson 6: CHOOSE ACTION vet options and plan			
What if I don't know what path to choose to move forward?			
How can I tell if an option is good for me?			
How do I make a simple plan?			
How do I know it's the right time to make a decision?			
What if I make the wrong decision?			
How can I be sure I am doing the right thing?			
How can I improve my chances of this being a good decision?			
Does saying thank you really make a difference?			
Why should I be grateful for something I haven't received yet?			
Lesson 7: CHOOSE CHANGE own your decision			
How do I know if I'm 'there' yet?			
What do I do after I get what I want?			
Lesson 8: When YOU are the decision coach			
When is it ok for me to decide for my significant other or family member?			
Can my kids learn complex decision making?			
How can I teach my kids about decision making?			
How can I teach my kids to be good decision makers?			
Closing: You leveled up!			
Are there checklists or templates I can use?			
Can I tell if my decision dexterity has improved now that I've taken this online course?			
How can I learn more?			

ABOUT THE AUTHOR
TERRIE is a business systems analyst and made a career facilitating software development teams through the thousands of decisions needed to deliver products to market.
She developed a unique framework that integrates both analysis and intuition, allowing decisions to come from a position of personal choice.

ABOUT THE ILLUSTRATOR
LYNN MARIE is an artist, tattooer, and owner of Rosewater Custom Tattooing in Portland, Oregon.

Books by Terrie Novak

Doodle and Decide is a companion to *Decision Dexterity, How to Overcome the Agony of Indecision*. This is ideal for readers who prefer to read *Decision Dexterity* in e-book format and still want to participate in the hands-on activities.

Decision Dexterity, the Online Course, provides content in video and audio format and has a complete library of downloadable digital files of the images and worksheets.
Enroll @terrienovak.com.

Terrie Novak   Lynn Marie

www.ingramcontent.com/pod-product-compliance
Lightning Source LLC
Chambersburg PA
CBHW081407070526
44583CB00020B/2711